# YOUR KNOWLEDGE HAS

- We will publish your bachelor's and
  master's thesis, essays and papers

- Your own eBook and book -
  sold worldwide in all relevant shops

- Earn money with each sale

Upload your text at www.GRIN.com
and publish for free

M. Riechert, A. Alredainy, J. Beierer, M. Christoffels, T. Falconer

# Improving Advertisement Efficiency with Information Systems Design

GRIN Publishing

**Bibliographic information published by the German National Library:**

The German National Library lists this publication in the National Bibliography; detailed bibliographic data are available on the Internet at http://dnb.dnb.de .

This book is copyright material and must not be copied, reproduced, transferred, distributed, leased, licensed or publicly performed or used in any way except as specifically permitted in writing by the publishers, as allowed under the terms and conditions under which it was purchased or as strictly permitted by applicable copyright law. Any unauthorized distribution or use of this text may be a direct infringement of the author s and publisher s rights and those responsible may be liable in law accordingly.

**Imprint:**

Copyright © 2010 GRIN Verlag, Open Publishing GmbH
Print and binding: Books on Demand GmbH, Norderstedt Germany
ISBN: 978-3-640-91288-9

**This book at GRIN:**

http://www.grin.com/en/e-book/171759/improving-advertisement-efficiency-with-information-systems-design

## GRIN - Your knowledge has value

Since its foundation in 1998, GRIN has specialized in publishing academic texts by students, college teachers and other academics as e-book and printed book. The website www.grin.com is an ideal platform for presenting term papers, final papers, scientific essays, dissertations and specialist books.

## Visit us on the internet:

http://www.grin.com/

http://www.facebook.com/grincom

http://www.twitter.com/grin_com

# Queensland University of Technology

## INB124 Information System Development

## Assessment 2

### Due Date: 22/10/2010

### Team Members:

| | |
|---|---|
| N6446906 | Abdalziz Alredainy |
| N6905544 | Jack Beierer |
| N5470846 | Mathew Christoffels |
| N7638604 | Mathias Riechert |
| N6369995 | Thomas Falconer |

# i.    Declaration by group members

Throughout this assignment the 'Real Team' agrees to a number of terms in order to maintain group cohesion and produce the best possible result. The terms refer to abiding by the QUT Academic Honesty System, developing and maintaining a strong team culture and to complete all distributed tasks to each member's full potential.

As a team we fully support and recognise the importance of academic honesty and agree to ensure that our work is our own. All quotes and sources will be formally referenced and acknowledged where due. Each team member has agreed to comply with in house team rules. This means maintaining regular communication, completing all given work and creating a friendly and professional team environment

By signing this declaration we agree to the aforementioned terms.


Abdalziz Alredainy              _____


Jack Beierer                    _____


Mathew Christoffels             _____


Mathias Riechert                _____


Thomas Falconer                 _____


Date                    03/09/2010

## i.     Executive Summary

This report has been created to successfully analyse a business problem and create the idea for an information system solution to that problem. The business problem chosen is that advertising for businesses is currently ineffective and could be improved thoroughly. Interactive advertising can successfully improve business advertising and therefore the design of ContAD was created. The idea of ContAD was created for users to connect with the content of business advertisements.

ContAD is an interactive advertisement system consisting of a variety of interactive advertising nodes. The advertising nodes are a user-friendly and interactive way of allowing customers to view and search through store deals and advertisements. The interactive advertising nodes consist of a touch screen that provides advertisements of the nearby shop deals. If a user likes a deal the advertising node can provide the user with a direct map to the store, and similar stores on that route. The system is needed because it will successfully improve the business problem that is ineffective advertising.

Throughout this report a number of areas will be covered consisting of: the different types of methodologies but more specifically the chosen waterfall methdology. The design of the project, the team member roles and the project and team dynamics. The information system, the theory regarding the need for the system, the basic idea of the system, the conceptual design of the system and finally a user guide for the system.

There are a variety of findings from the analysis of the business problem and the creation of the interactive advertising system ContAD. These findings consist of:

- Advertising in its current form is ineffective and therefore could be improved
- Interactive advertising is the way of the future and will take over current advertising
- ContAD will successfully use interactive advertising to improve the business problem discussed

# Contents

# 1 Introduction

Information systems are the, "arrangement of people, data, processes, information presentation and information technology to support and improve day-to-day operations in a business" (Chan, 2010). In terms of the purpose of this report, the information system is technology based and the aim of the report is to successfully create an information system to solve an important business problem. Furthermore, the significance of the report is to understand problems that businesses face and to develop, create and market a valid information system to meet the needs of the business.

The main assumption made while building this report are that nodes are a current form of interaction in public places such as airports. However, the proposed information system has used node technology to allow users to interact with advertising.

The report layout will consist of an overview of the conduct of the report including the systems development methodologies. Following this is the information system consisting of the theoretical basis, business problem analysis, basic idea of the system, conceptual design of the system and a user guide of the system. The conclusion will consist of a summary of the main findings of the report. Finally, a list of the assumptions made for the assignment will be discussed.

# 2 Overview of the conduct of the report

### 2.1.1 Systems Development Methodologies

Today, Software Development can mean the success or failure of a business. At a planning and design level, it is critical to have a clear and quality development methodology in place. 'A methodology represents a package of practical ideas and proven practices for a given area of activity, such as the planning, design development or management of IT-based systems.' (INTOSAI, 2008)

More accurately, Software Development Methodology allows the user to define a set of instructions or guidelines when designing and developing their system. This framework is based on a wide range of methodologies available. More common methods in use today are The Waterfall Model, Star Method, Rapid Application Development (RAD) and the Joint Application Method (JAD).

### 2.1.2 Detailed Systems Development Methodologies

Each method is unique and has its own strengths and weaknesses. More importantly it is how these strengths and weaknesses are put into place that will determine the integrity and success of the user's system. The Star method uses an individual approach by evaluating the system at every level. 'Evaluation is central to designing interactive systems. Everything gets evaluated at every step of the process' (Chan, 2010). The other interesting aspect to point out is that the Star Method can start at any point and the activities can occur in any order. The Waterfall method uses a systematic approach where each phase is completed before the next. RAD Methodology works by speeding up the software development process using a system of informal communication, reusing current systems and testing early prototypes. In all, it is a 'concept where products can be developed faster and of higher quality' (Search Software Quality 2008). Lastly the JAD method 'is a methodology that involves the client or end user in the design and development of an application, through a succession of collaborative workshops called JAD sessions as stated by Search Software Quality (2007).

Because the scope of work for the project is not large, the best idea is to keep the process simple. The Star method is not suitable for this small scale approach because its framework can become complex due to various possible start points. The RAD methodology asks for a rushed and less detailed method. As the team are inexperienced and new to the learning's of Systems and Software Development, it is best to take a more cautious and timely approach to the project. As discussed earlier, the JAD methodology requires interaction with clients and end users. This project is conceptually based; as a result there are no real clients or end users. This approach could have been possible using fellow students and the public as fake clients, but the team feels the opinions and knowledge of these people would be invalid or not at a meaningful and detailed level required.

### 2.1.3 The Waterfall Methodology

After evaluating all the aforementioned methodologies by looking deep into their respective approaches and processes, it was decided that the best methodology to develop the interactive advertisement system is the 'Waterfall Methodology'.

The Waterfall's clear, simple and systematic approach to systems development was the deciding factor in choosing this methodology. This framework will allow 'The Real' team to create a set of manageable tasks at each sequential stage of development. This is important to the team because it provides a clear goal and means we cannot move onto the next phase until we have agreed upon a successful completion of the current phase. Another aspect of the Waterfall Methodology that appealed to the team is its ability to remain clear and structured. This suits our team, as we are inexperienced system developers who will rely on a set of guidelines throughout the project. The only issue with this method is its inflexibility. The framework is designed to be sequential; therefore we cannot skip ahead to other aspects of the project, depicted by Figure 5.

The Waterfall Methodology 'is considered the classic approach to the systems development life cycle. The waterfall model describes a development method that is linear and sequential' (Search Software Quality, 2008). The Waterfall framework is designed to keep each stage of development manageable by breaking down 'an orderly sequence of development steps to help ensure the adequacy of documentation and design reviews to ensure the quality, reliability, and maintainability of the developed software' (Principle based Project Management, 2007).

The stages of development in their simplest form are as follows:

**Requirements** – understanding the task/problem at hand and developing a list of requirements needed to begin

**Design** – developing a conceptual then physical design of the system

**Implementation** – putting the physical design of the system into practice

**Verification** – does the system work as it should (testing) and does it solve the problem as detailed in the requirements stage

**Maintenance** – continual testing, maintenance and updates of the system

## 2.2 Key steps undertaken in the design project

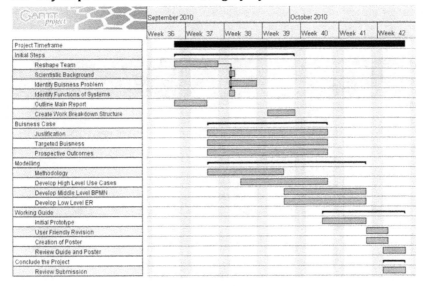

**Figure 1 Work Breakdown Structure**

Figure 1 depicts the work breakdown structure for the project. This particular structure emphasises time given to create a correct and complete business case for the project. This is an important focus as a clearly defined business case can lead to a successful project and keeping the project development focused on achieving the business goal (Moore, 2009).

## 2.3 Team members and their role in the project

Below are the key roles available within the project. These are conducted by one or more team members. The descriptions of each role show the direct responsibilities that are accounted for in the project.

| Role | Responsibilities | Team member |
|---|---|---|
| **Editor** | <ul><li>Check for Grammar & Spelling,</li><li>Ensure the report is written in Scientistic style, that all aspects are presented by logic and research,</li><li>Make sure that the content contributors include all Citations when appropriate,</li><li>Make sure that referenced works are included in the bibliography,</li><li>Track team meetings minutes, and</li><li>Make sure every paragraph conforms to properly written English.</li></ul> | Jack & Mathias |
| **Team Manager** | <ul><li>Organize Team into work roles,</li><li>Split work in separate blocks where appropriate,</li><li>Resolve conflicts within the team,</li><li>Analyse the performance of the team and adjust working schedule of the project,</li><li>Participation in design process, and</li><li>Providing guidance to other work areas that match the project plan.</li></ul> | Mathew |
| **Designer** | <ul><li>Generate user centred design requirements (What is needed by the user),</li><li>Design a Graphical User Interface that matches prior requirements,</li><li>Develop the Project Poster,</li><li>Actively participate in the design process, and</li><li>Detail content generated by the design aspects of the project.</li></ul> | Aziz & Mathias |
| **Developer** | <ul><li>Participate in the generation of user centred requirements,</li><li>Participation in the design process,</li><li>Explain the models in textual format for the report,</li><li>Provide a comparison on alterative possible methods for the project, and</li><li>Write user documentation, supported by other team member roles.</li></ul> | Tom |

**Table 1 Team member roles**

## 2.4 Project and team dynamics

The project flow starts with the Designer. Their goal is to identify the design requirements of the targeted users of the project. Once these requirements are specified, they are passed onto the Developer and Editor. The Designer will also help build other areas of the project, passing them onto the Developer and Editor as well. In order to keep the Designer's objectives accurate, work may be reviewed by the team leader.

In the Developer role team members actively participate in generating models and information relevant to achieving the project's goals. Requirements (and other identified processes) sent from the Designer are built into models reflecting the project's needs. Work conducted here is passed to the Editor role for review. The performance of the developer role is reviewed by the team leader which ensures the progress of the project is on track and that conflicts or errors are investigated.

An Editor's primary objective is to review all possible documentation before it is submitted into the main project document. They check for accuracy in the work as well as ensuring a high level of cohesion between aspects of the project.

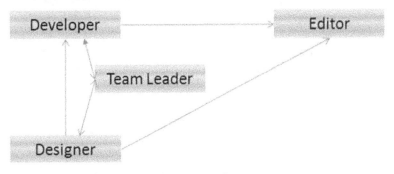

Figure 2 Team Roles

Under the Team Manager role, team members investigate the process of the project and its relevance to the project goal. Other team roles rely on the Team Manager to provide direction in the project and mid-progress reviews of tasks, before they go to the editors. This role utilizes communication in both directions – to and from other team member roles.

In summary, the flow of information between the roles allows for high accuracy of work. Errors and inconsistencies can be caught by the editors while the team leader is able to effectively manage the project's progress.

## 2.5  Conduct conclusion

Using a System Software Development Methodology is an excellent advantage when undertaking a software system projects. They provide a user with quality guidelines and aid in developing a clear goal. While researching the many available tools to guide the project full respect was paid to each methodology that was suitable to our problem. After detailing through each framework, it was evident that the Waterfall method was most appropriate to our team.

The key steps to go through the design process are shown in Figure 1 Work Breakdown Structure and include theoretical analysis, business analysis, modelling, creating a working guide and the final paper editing steps. Accomplishing the key milestones in time is crucial for achieving the best possible quality in designing and writing disciplines.

The team members were designated different roles in the project; these are depicted in Figure 2 Team Roles. The work is broken down into roles to gain individual responsibilities in the project, leading to a higher quality of the final text. The team and project dynamics are defined to specify how the work is organized.

# 3 The Information System

## 3.1 Interactive Advertisement System- theoretical basis

Advertisements are a "matter which is published or broadcast via internet, direct mail, point of sale, packaging or direct distribution to individuals which draws the attention of the public or a segment of it to a product, service, person, organisation or line of conduct in a manner calculated to promote or oppose directly or indirectly to the product, service, person, organisation or line of conduct" (Belch, 2008). There are different forms of advertisements known: TV advertisements, the radio, Internet advertising and the outdoor advertising. While print billboards have been the mainstay of outdoor advertising in the past, the addition of electronic signs is just beginning to take off (Brill, 2010). As a result, the decision which medium is suited best depends heavily on the customer group and if the target usage area is inside or outside.

For outside usage various forms of billbords have to be considered: Electronic light-emitting diode (LED) billboards offer a greater flexibility than conventional billboards with high brightness and resolution. LED screens are an integrated display system, which combines microelectronic technology, photonic technology, computer technology and information processing technology (Technology for the World, 2010). LED billboards have a variety of advantages over regular billboards in that they can provide animations and essentially are TV advertisements outdoors. They can also be changed with the click of a button from an external location rather than sending out crews to pull down the messages (Brill, 2010). In terms of statistics, after a vibrating mascara brush was advertised in a Japanese subway, Japan's Toppan Printing stated that, "commuters were approximately 50% more likely to look at electronic paper with a moving image when compared to their static equivalents" (PSFK, 2009). There are a variety of benefits LED Giant Displays can provide for outdoor advertising, these consist of:

- Moving Messages - have been proven to catch the human eye's attention up to 8 times more that a static advertising billboard
- Higher Brightness - which allows the LED Billboard to stand out of the crowd both during the day and at night
- Increasing LED Resolution - that is transforming the outdoor screens in HUGE high-resolution TV monitors
- Videos and Animations Capabilities - that allows to broadcast TV commercial as seen on television
- Multiple Message Provider - that allows advertising companies to run multiple campaigns on the same screens
- PC Remote Control - so you can change the ads in just a mouse click rather than sending out a crew to pull down and replace a billboard message. (Euro Display, 2006)

For indoor advertising an interesting approach is described by Rakkolainen and Lugmayr (Rakkolainen & Lugmayr, 2007) and uses fog to project the content on it. By tracking the viewer interaction with the content is possible. It is more interactive than traditional forms of advertisement because touching and walking through the content is possible. The main disadvantage is the use of a projector because that causes the restriction of only being used indoors. That leads to the decision to use screens without projectors, because they are more flexible for outdoor usage. The tracking aspect still seems very promising to increase interaction.

Models can be used as a guideline how to create a good advertisement. The first model to be described is the AIDA model (Attention, Interest, Desire and Action) by E. St. Elmo Lewis in 1898 (Vakratsas & Ambler, 1999). These steps build the foundation of the Design process described below.

Interactive advertisement "may contain content of multiple media types such as text, image, flash, video, or mixture of these formats." Furthermore "there is a functional extension to the advertisement by the aid of existing communication technologies, such as Voice over Internet Protocol (VoIP), short message service (SMS), and email, which allows consumers to participate actively in the interactions with the advertisement content" (Zhang, Ma, & Sun, 2008). The interaction becomes a central design aspect. Consequently analyzing Human Computer Interaction (HCI) is neccessairy.

Human Computer Interaction is concerned with the design, evaluation, and implementation of interactive computing systems for human use (Baecker, 1995). To ensure that every aspect of the interaction process is dealt with sufficently, these user interface elements are considered:

| Key aspect | Description | Examples |
|---|---|---|
| Mental models | structures or organizations of data, functions, tasks, roles, and people in groups at work or play. | Content, function, media, tool, role, goal, and task hierarchies |
| Navigation | movement through the mental models, i.e., throughcontent and tools. | Dialogue techniques such as menus, windows, dialogue boxes, control panels, icons, and tool palettes. |
| Interaction | input/output techniques, including feedback | Choices of keyboards, mice, pens, or microphones for input; the choices of visual display screens, loudspeakers, or headsets for output; and the use of drag-and drop selection/action sequences. |
| Appearance | visual, auditory, and tactile characteristics, i.e., perceptual attributes | Choices of colors, fonts, verbal style (e.g., verbose/terse or informal/formal), sound cues, and vibration modes. |
| Metaphors | fundamental concepts communicated via words, images, sounds, and tactile experiences. | Concepts of pages, shopping carts, chatrooms, and blogs |

Table 2: Human Computer Interaction key elements[1]

---
[1] (Marcus, 2002)

The key elements build a hierarchy as shown in Figure 3. The mental models build the basis for the navigation. The interactions of the system depend on the navigation, and the Metaphors can be discussed effectively after all necessary appearance discussion is done.

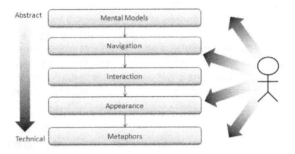

Figure 3: User centred Human Computer Interaction process

To be successful in the area of advertisement the User Interface has to be tailored specifically for the user. In the design process the focus on the user will be the highest priority.

## 3.2 Business Problem Analysis

Advertising is an important way for any business to succeed. Businesses inside shopping malls and airports currently face the challenge of close competition (Bezjian-Avery, Calder, & Iacobucci, 1998). Effective advertising is an important factor in the success of these businesses due to the reason that there are a variety of stores nearby selling the same type of products. The problem that these businesses face is that traditional advertising is not as effective as it could be and is currently on a solid decline. (Chertkova, 2008) While traditionally still paper advertising has been the common trend for most businesses, interactive advertising systems are the vision for the future of advertising.

The advertising nodes are able to present a form of interactive advertisements. This type of advertisement will increase the customer's involvement and satisfaction while providing options for customer feedback, which further drives the advertisements to be more relevant to the customer (Pavlou & Stewart, 2000). As interactive media is an inherently communication to and from the customer, it allows businesses utilizing the proposed advertisement nodes to adapt the advertisement to make it more effective and invoke better responses from the customer. This type of rich media typically doubles the chances of a sale, while tripling the chances of getting further interest for information from the customer (Digital Media, 2010).

Expansion into new digital technologies provides new opportunities to gain a business advantage when investing in digital advertisements compared to traditional methods. Through the deployment of advertisement nodes, these expanding options are made available for business advantages to be gained.

Furthermore, interactive media is a successful solution to the business problem of ineffective advertising for current businesses.

## 3.3 The basic design idea of the system

ContAD: connectivity, content and advertising is the outline for an interactive advertisement system consisting of a variety of interactive advertising nodes. The advertising nodes are a user-friendly and interactive way of allowing customers to view and search through store deals and advertisements. The interactive advertising nodes consist of a touch screen that provides advertisements of the nearby shop deals, advertisements, transportation hubs, maps. The underlying database is capable of handling variable data types by mapping the fields depending on the content. If a user likes a deal the advertising node can provide the user with a direct map to the store, and similar stores on that route.

Interactive advertisement nodes are networked with a second type of node - view only. View only advertisement nodes are located throughout shopping malls, airports and bus stops both indoor and outdoor. The most popular advertisements and contents from the interactive advertising nodes are shown on the view only advertisement nodes to attract further customers. The decision which content is "popular" is realized by data mining algorithms.

The interactive advertising nodes also have facial recognition through a built-in camera to remember the user and his or her preferences. Therefore, when users return to an interactive advertising node similar deals and offers will be displayed.

The advertisements displayed on the system are created by the advertisement partners. Once they are created or modified they are then sent to the advertisement management system for review. The time date can be chosen for when the new advertisement will start being shown and the advertisement management system will update it accordingly. Once the new advertisements are reviewed successfully, they are uploaded to the main database for all advertisement nodes to access and use.

The approach of placing the advertising node will be in public place such as shopping malls, tourism area and crowded public areas. Shopping malls are one of the good examples for the advertising node to be installed for the reason that it is filled with a lot of people who are looking for information. Also, the tourism region and crowded public areas are excellent locations to install and put up an advertising node for the reason that it is mostly a new area for many people who come from different places seeking information about the area. Generally advertising nodes will be installed in locations and areas that attract large numbers of customers. The abilities and the feature of the advertising node should be visible to the user who is seeking information.

In summary it can be said, therefore, that the system offers more interaction and recognition functionality than conventional advertisement nodes. The higher interactivity is used to attract more customers to use the nodes. This makes it more attractive for advertisement partners to use the dynamic advertisement options provided by the system. Furthermore the customers can search for any data type defined by the system, and gain more information they need in the individual situation.

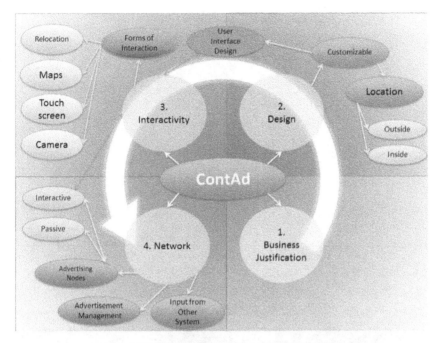

**Figure 4: Mind Map showing the system of the ContAd outline**

The mind map demonstrates the outline of ContAD. It depicts the basic idea of the system in an easy to understand model. The business justification is expressed in section 3.2 and formulates the design of the system. After the system is designed, the interactivity between the user and the system is defined in detail. Finally, the network was created to allow the variety of different parties to interact with ContAD.

## 3.4 The conceptual design of the system

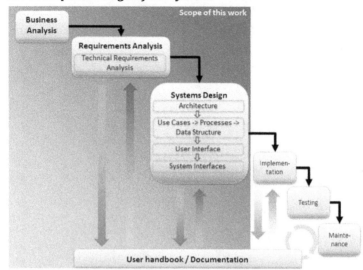

**Figure 5 Waterfall model with sub processes**

| Step | | Page |
|------|------|------|
| Business Analysis | The business Analysis includes the problem analysis and the basic idea. | 10-13 |
| Requirements Analysis | The requirements analysis defines technical requirements detailed. | 14 |
| Systems Design | The Architecture, the Use Cases -> Processes -> Data structures, User Interface, and System Interfaces are described in the systems design step. | 17-27 |
| User Handbook | The user handbook describes the basic functionalities. | 28 |

**Table 3 Conceptual Design references**

Figure 5 shows the extended waterfall model on the basis of the waterfall methodology discussed in Chapter 2.1.3. The initial step of business analysis is preceding the requirements analysis to outline the business problem and how the ContAD addresses the occurring problems. Table 3 shows on which page the steps are discussed detailed.

## 3.4.1 Technical Requirements Analysis

In order to comprehend the technical requirements of the system, there are several considerations that need to be made. People that use the system are broken up into specific categories below, based on their level of interaction. Following on is a list of users, systems and actions that can be taken.

**Viewers** are individuals whom passively use the Advertisement Node. They either view an advertisement (or feature) from the node but do not actively interact with it. This is the same interaction for traditional advertising, where the only action that can be used with traditional advertising is to view it.

After viewing some information on the node, they can either choose to leave the node alone or interact with the node. If a viewer interacts with the Advertisement Node, they become information seekers.

**Information Seekers** are individuals whom use interactive functionality of the advertising nodes to get more information. The types of interactions they can use include being able to find an advertisement on the node, get directions to shop or request support at that Advertisement Node. Information seekers have a longer exposure to Advertisement Nodes than viewers.

**Advertising Partners** supply the content of advertisements for the Advertisement Nodes to display. They do this by interacting with the advertisement management system to upload new information and advertisements. Advertising Partners may view their advertisements on an Advertisement Node, in which case they are also Viewers. If they interact with the Advertisement Node by using one of its functions, then they become Information Seekers, in addition to being an Advertising Partner.

**Technicians** primarily support Advertisement Nodes by performing maintenance on them when required. Their goal is to ensure that Advertisement Nodes are operational and run smoothly. These individuals utilize information provided by the network to make changes and take action when required.

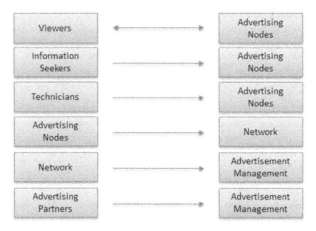

**Figure 6: Connection between objects**

These single connections have to be summed up in a resulting diagram. Figure 6 shows this connection and makes all paths visible. It is the basis for the network model and architecture in the following chapters.

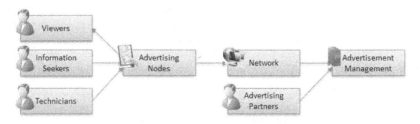

**Figure 7: All connection paths combined**

There are a variety of different types of advertisement systems used. These consist of: Advertisement Nodes, Network Infrastructure and Advertisement Management, all of which are depicted in Figure 7. Furthermore, the model demonstrates the connection paths of the different parties involved.

| Element | Interactions with | Actions that can be taken |
|---|---|---|
| **Viewers** | Advertisement Nodes | View an Ad<br>Ability to detect motion<br>Ability to show help |
| **Information Seekers** | Advertisement Nodes | View an Ad<br>Ability to show maps<br>Ability to find locations<br>Ability to give directions<br>Ability to search Ads<br>Ability to capture person's details (history, image/camera)<br>Ability to record and analyse voice<br>Ability to 'like' an Ad<br>Request Support |
| **Technicians** | Advertisement Nodes | Access maintenance mode<br>Establish external connection<br>Update the system<br>Find GPS location |
| **Advertisement Nodes** | Network | Connect to Network<br>Receive data<br>Transmit statistics<br>Report Problem<br>Update user history |
| **Network** | Advertisement Management | Establish connections<br>Locate Advertisement Nodes<br>Transmit Data |
| **Advertisement Partners** | Advertisement Management | Upload new Ad<br>Remove Ad<br>Change Ad Properties<br>View Ad Statistics<br>Pay for Ad<br>Request Support |

**Table 4 User interactions and the functions associated**

Table 4 above demonstrates the user interactions with ContAD and the functions associated. The advertisement partners only require a computer or a laptop and the ability to create new advertisements and modify old ones. Once this has been achieved they need the internet to send the advertisement to advertisement management. After the advertisement management has received the updated advertisement it will update it into the system according to the time stamp.

## 3.4.2 Architecture of the Information System

Software Architecture is a purposeful design plan of a system that describes the elements of a system, how they interact in order to meet the systems requirements. They can be designed in several ways, depending on the purpose and requirements of the system (Hofmeister, Nordt, & Soni, 2000). The requirements analysis in chapter 3.4.1 show that there is a necessity for a distributed system, because different user groups have to access the same data. A monolithic system would not meet the access requirements. The basic approach is to divide the interface, the application and the data storage into separate parts. Figure 8 shows the basic C/S Architectures.

(1)  Presentation + Application + Data Storage in one System
(2)  Presentation is separated, Application + Data Storage in one System
(3)  Presentation + Application in one System, Data Storage is separated
(4)  Presentation + Application + Data Storage in one System

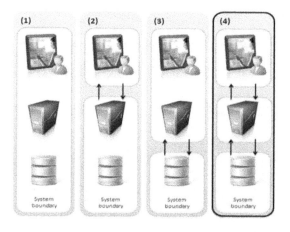

**Figure 8: Basic C/S Architectures**

Each separation increases the complexity because more communication has to be handled. The analysis in Chapter 3.4.1 shows that many different actors need to interact with the same application system to access the database. So only (2) and (4) are possible for the system. (4) is more flexible for future changes because different databases can be accessed by the system. The chosen architecture therefore has to be a 3-tier Client Server Architecture. Furthermore a data interface to advertisement partners should be available for data import.

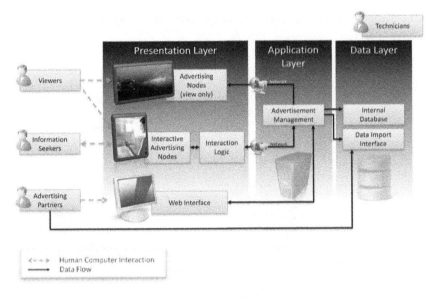

**Figure 9: ContAD Architecture**

Figure 9 shows the architecture plan based on the paths identified in the requirements analysis (See Figure 7 in chapter 3.4.1). The process still has to be adjusted to meet the requirements of a 3-tier architecture. The Indoor interaction nodes are no pure presentation devices because the interactivity performs not satisfactory on a website interface. The presentation logic layer is represented by the "Interaction Logic" in the diagram. For the Outdoor Nodes and the Advertising Partner Interface web / network access is sufficient. The central point of the system is the Application Layer which handles the allocation of the advertisement data from the internal database and the communication between the other devices. The Data Manipulation layer is included in the application layer, as it is handled in the same program. As a result of this step the further design process concentrates on showing the functionality of the interaction logic and the Advertisement Management before giving switching to the user interface aspects.

### 3.4.3 Information about use cases, supported processes and data structure

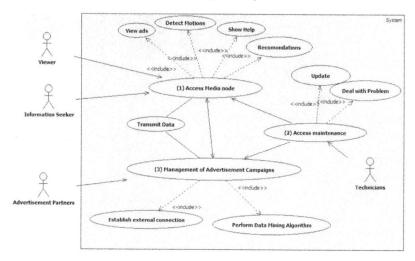

**Figure 10 Use Case Diagram**

Figure 10 shows the Use Case Diagram for the ContAD system. The actors identified in the requirements analysis and are connected to the main use cases. The included subcases are included to show a more detailed level of function. The Access media node is the core of the design process. It includes all functions dealing access to data stored in the database. Furthermore it adds user centred functions like help. This functionality is modelled in the "Interactive Advertising Node" swimlane in Figure 11 System Connectivity Model on page 20.

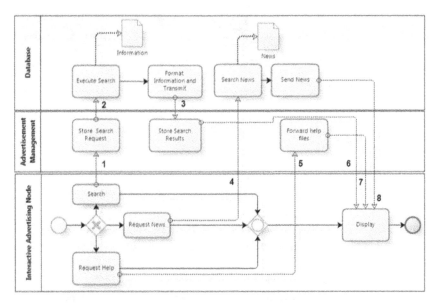

**Figure 11 System Connectivity Model**

This model depicts how the system handles input from an Interactive Advertisement Node. Once a process is started, it has three primary options to choose from. The first is to Search. This requests information, which may be advertising or store details. A request is sent to Advertisement Management, which stores that search in a search history. Forwarding the request forward, the database runs a search for the requested information. The results get stored by Advertisement Management to provide useful system statistics. Lastly that information is sent back to the Interactive Advertisement Node to be displayed.

The process for Request News is very similar to Search except that the initial request is not stored by Advertisement Management. Request Help is a function typically used by Information Seekers. A request for information is passed to Advertisement Management, they keep track of helpful information. The data is sent back to the display, resulting in a very quick process.

| Transfer | Function | Sending From | Receiving At | Data Type |
|---|---|---|---|---|
| 1 | Search | Int. Advertisement Node | Advertisement Management | Text |
| 2 | Store Search Request | Advertisement Management | Database | Text |
| 3 | Format Information and Transmit | Database | Advertisement Management | Information |
| 4 | Request News | Int. Advertisement Node | Database | Token |

| Transfer | Function | Sending From | Receiving At | Data Type |
|----------|----------|--------------|--------------|-----------|
| 5 | Request Help | Int. Advertisement Node | Advertisement Management | Token |
| 6 | Store Search Results | Advertisement Management | Int. Advertisement Node | Information |
| 7 | Forward Help Files | Advertisement Management | Int. Advertisement Node | Help Info |
| 8 | Send News | Database | Int. Advertisement Node | News |

**Transfer 1 – Search**

For this data transfer, text is sent from the Information Advertisement Node to Advertisement Management. This text could be a name of a store or a unique identifier for an advertisement.

**Transfer 2 – Store Search Request**

In this function the same data that was transferred to Advertisement Management in Transfer 1, is forwarded to the Database. This information is used to run a new process within the Database called Execute Search.

**Transfer 3 – Format Information and Transmit**

This process takes the information found in the database from Execute Search and compiles it into a format that can be displayed by Interactive Advertisement Node.

**Transfer 4 – Request News**

An Interactive Advertisement Node can send a specially crafted token to Database. This token is built with a special string of text and numbers that is unique. When Database receives this token, it knows to execute Search News.

**Transfer 5 – Request Help**

Like Request News, Request Help utilizes a specially crafted token, different to the one used for News. This token is sent to Advertisement Management to request current help files.

**Transfer 6 – Store Search Results**

Store Search Results is an intermediary step. This process forwards information from the database to an Interactive Advertisement Node.

**Transfer 7 – Forward Help Files**

Advertisement Management sends a copy of the help files to an Advertisement Node. As this data may contain text, images and videos, the help info data-type is used.

**Transfer 8 – Send News**

When the Database sends news to an Advertisement Node, it is in a special type of data called 'News'. Like the 'Help Info' data-type, this may contain text, images and video components.

### 3.4.4 Relevant interfaces to other system where required

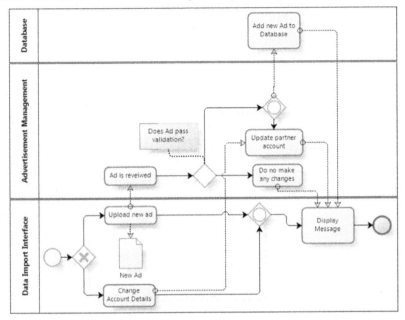

**Figure 12 BPMN Model of Data Input**

Advertisement partners require external access to the advertisement system. This access allows advertisement partners to accomplish two things – update their account details and upload new advertisement materials. As shown above in Figure 12 when new data is uploaded, it goes through a review stage. This allows staff members to review the content for appropriateness and alter the advertisement partner if there are changes required.

If the ad is reviewed successfully, it is immediately added to the database and the account details for the advertisement partner are updated. This is so that the advertisement partner can keep track of their advertisements and be charged correctly. Under all circumstances the advertisement partner will receive a message notification of the success or failure of the task. Based on that structure an ERM is designed to show the database layout:

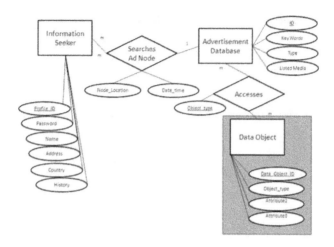

**Figure 13 Entity Relationship Model**

Figure 13 depicts an Entity Relationship Model describing the basic process of ContAD. It shows how each system is tied together and their direct relationships. The Data Object is an abstract data table. That means that the names of the fields are mapped on the columns as shown in the next figure.

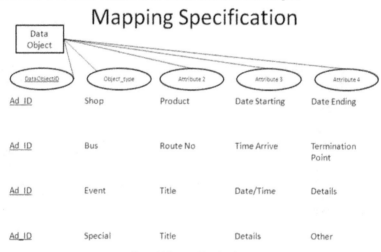

**Figure 14 System Mapping Specs**

Figure 14 illustrates an example of the Attributes of each Ad type. It is important the system database recognises different types of data and their details.

### 3.4.5 A user interface

The foundation for the user interface design process is the information outlined by the elements of Human Computer Interaction described by Markus (2002). Many of the steps to describe Human Computer Interaction are described earlier in the process of the design. The focus of this section focus on extending the technical view on the steps already taken by the graphical aspects.

**Mental Models** include content, function, media, tool, role, goal, and task hierarchies. In section 3.4.3 the Use Case diagram shows the basic content. The Business Process Models give a more detailed view on the topic. The ERD shows the data hierarchy on the lowest level.

**Navigation** includes the movement through the models and tools. Figure 7: All connection paths combined shows all navigation paths between the interaction objects. On that basis 3 different HCI - interface types are identified: Interactive Advertising Nodes need to enable the user to interact with a system. The touch screen technology described in the introduction needs to be supported by them. Advertising Nodes are for viewing only and work like conventional digital screens. The third way of interacting is the web interface for uploading advertisement data by the advertisement partners.

**Interaction** is one of the key aspects to increase user acceptance. The most intuitive way of interacting is achieved by providing a touchscreen interface. The interface must be as simple, easy and visual as possible. According to Few the highest acceptance is achieved when simplicity is used for graphical and textual objects (Few, 2006). That means showing as few pixels as possible, reduce unnecessary pixels (lines, 3d elements, etc.) and show only objects which hold information. For our approach this rule is only partly usable, because attracting the customer's attention by advertisement requires many advertisement objects. No keyboards, mice or microphones are used for the system. Using audio as a way to get attention from by walking customers can be used optionally.

**Appearance** includes all graphical considerations. The rules for the design are derived from Few (2006) using the law of simplicity as the basic principle.

| Appearance category | Inclusion details |
|---|---|
| Colour | The colour scheme is based on the colour red. In the triad colour scheme approach the colours blue and yellow are used in different variations to give make the interface look balanced. 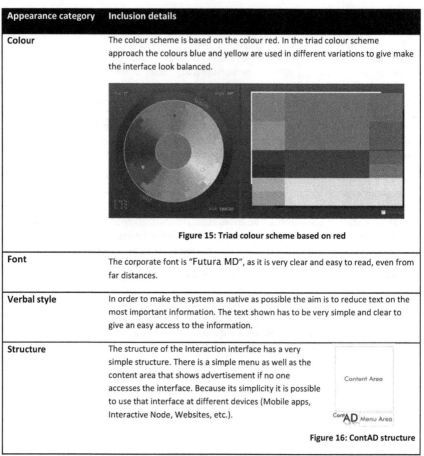 Figure 15: Triad colour scheme based on red |
| Font | The corporate font is "Futura MD", as it is very clear and easy to read, even from far distances. |
| Verbal style | In order to make the system as native as possible the aim is to reduce text on the most important information. The text shown has to be very simple and clear to give an easy access to the information. |
| Structure | The structure of the Interaction interface has a very simple structure. There is a simple menu as well as the content area that shows advertisement if no one accesses the interface. Because its simplicity it is possible to use that interface at different devices (Mobile apps, Interactive Node, Websites, etc.). Content Area ContAD Menu Area Figure 16: ContAD structure |

Table 5: Appearance details

**Methaphors:**

Figure 17: Interface Design proposal

The interface for User – Interactive Advertisement node is based on the findings in the step above. It shows the menu and the content part. The menu includes the possibility to log into the system. A more detailed explanation is given in the user guide.

### 3.4.6 Relevant interfaces to other system where required

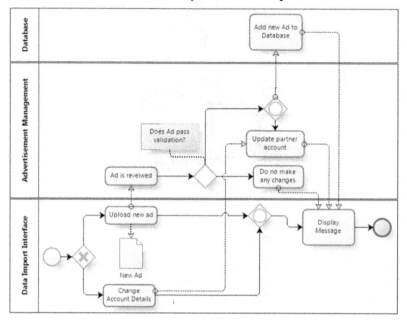

**Figure 18 BPMN Model of Data Input**

Advertisement partners require external access to the advertisement system. This access allows advertisement partners to accomplish two things – update their account details and upload new advertisement materials. As shown above in Figure 12 when new data is uploaded, it goes through a review stage. This allows staff members to review the content for appropriateness and alter the advertisement partner if there are changes required.

If the ad is reviewed successfully, it is immediately added to the database and the account details for the advertisement partner are updated. This is so that the advertisement partner can keep track of their advertisements and be charged correctly. Under all circumstances the advertisement partner will receive a message notification of the success or failure of the task.

## 3.5 The user guide to working with the system

ContAD is an interactive advertisement system that allows the user to view the hottest deals in the shops nearby. The user can use the search function to look for advertisements and deals. If a user enjoys an advertisement ContAD will provide a direct map to the store.

**Figure 19 Screen layout example**

**Search**

1. Click on the search button at the bottom right of the screen.
2. Use the digital keypad at the bottom of the screen to search for information.
3. Press OK.

The list of information will appear on the screen.

4. Select the information object.

The results will be displayed.

**Support**

1. Select the support button at the bottom right of the screen.

The user guide will be displayed on the screen.

2. Select which topic you need support with.

**Report a problem**

1. Select the 'report problem' button at the bottom right of the help screen.

A list of possible problems appear.

If the problem is on the list go to step 2, if not go to step 3.

2. Select the problem that has occurred with ContAD and a technician will be there the same day.
3. Select the 'other' button.

An empty box will appear.

4. Type what is wrong into the box.
5. Press OK.

**Login.**

1. Select the login button at the bottom right of the screen

Note: You cannot login to ContAD without making a profile; this can be achieved by selecting the profile button at the top right of the screen.

2. Align face with the picture frame and you will be logged in.

Note: If ContAD does not recognise the face go to step 3.

3. Login using your name and password.

**Profile**

1. Select the profile button at the bottom right of the screen.

A list of questions appears.

2. Answer the questions truthfully.
3. Above create profile select the facial recognition button.
4. Align your face to fit into the photo frame.
5. Select 'take picture'.

You will be re-directed back to the profile page.

6. Check to make sure the answers are correct.
7. Select 'create profile' at the bottom.
8. Once your profile has been created return to the main screen to login.

## 3.6  Information System Conclusion

The information system created consists of an idea for an interactive advertisement system. The theory for the system was researched from a variety of valid resources. This formed the basis for the business problem analysis. Furthermore, the basic idea of the system was created based on this research. The conceptual design of the system was then created including the technical requirements analysis, architecture of the interactive advertisement system, the different types of models developed, the user interface, other relevant interfaces to the other systems and a user guide for the system.

**Figure 20: ContAD Marketing**

## Conclusion

The structure of the report consists of an overview of the conduct of the report including the systems development methodologies. The system development methodology chosen was the waterfall methodology. It proved to be efficient for small projects. Because no implementation was included there were no redesigning steps required. For the realization of the project the switch to the spiral model is a good option to hande redesign issues. The team members were designated different roles in the project to ensure the smooth flow of the report. The roles built a good foundation to break up the work in separate tasks. Furthermore using this approach ensured that all of the three views (developer, designer, editor) are considered while going through the steps. The team dynamics express these roles more specifically and helped working together collaboratively.

The information system section outlines the business problem that businesses currently have ineffective advertising. Furthermore, the idea for an information system named ContAD has been created for users to connect them with the content of business advertisements. It also displays the conceptual design of the system and a user guide for the system.

The report successfully supported team work and task allocation as demonstrated by Figure 2. All members took different roles in completing the report.

Problematic is the high scope of the project. A specialization on a certain field of data would have reduced the complexity of the system but decrease the usefulness and efficiency of the product at the same time. Giving more information about other data but only advertisements increases the information potential for the customers using the device. Having one central point of information access increases the user acceptance and therefore makes the results of the advertisement more valuable.

The next steps are implementing and testing of the software based on the functionality described in the design process. If redesign is necessary a new cycle for the changes could be made. This would change the methodology to a spiral model. When the programming and testing is done the product can be introduced in the marked. Another possibility is to widen the scope of the work. The application presented could easily be converted to smartphone apps, making the information available inside of the mall for everyone on his mobile. The nodes can supply Wi-Fi for this app. The whole system is designed very flexible in make changes, customizations and adaptations easy to implement.

# 4 Bibliography

Baecker, R. M. (1995). *Readings in human-computer interaction: toward the year 2000.*

Balanced Scorecard Institute. (2010). *Balanced Scorecard Basics.* Retrieved October 17, 2010, from http://balancedscorecard.org

Belch, G. (2008). *Advertising and Promotion: An Integrated Marketing Communication Perspective.* McGraw-Hill Higher Education.

Bezjian-Avery, A., Calder, B., & Iacobucci, D. (1998). New media interactive advertising vs. traditional advertising. *Journal of advertising research, Vol. 38,* 23–32.

Brill, L. M. (2010). *LED Billboards: Outdoor Advertising in the Video Age.* Retrieved September 2010, from http://www.signindustry.com/led/articles/2002-07-30-LBledBillboards.php3

Chan, T. (2010). *INB124 Info Systems Development.* Retrieved October 12, 2010, from QUT Blackboard: http://blackboard.qut.edu.au/webapps/content/INB124

Chertkova, A. (2008, December 1). *Traditional vs. Internet Advertising in 2009?* Retrieved Septemeber 23, 2010, from 77 Lab: http://lab.77agency.com/marketing-analysis/traditional-vs-internet-advertising-in-2009-873/

Digital Media. (2010, July 23). *What drives automative advertising?* Retrieved September 23, 2010, from Digital Media: http://www.digital-media.net.au/article/what-drives-automotive-advertising/520776.aspx

Euro Display. (2006). *The "Outdoor Electronic Advertising" Advantage.* Retrieved September 2010, from http://www.ledscreensexpert.com/2006/11/12/the-outdoor-electronic-advertising-advantage/

Exinfm. (2002). *Excellene In Finance.* Exinfm.

Few, S. (2006). *Information dashboard design.* O'Reilly Media, Inc.

Hofmeister, C., Nordt, R., & Soni, D. (2000). *Applied software architecture.* Addison-Wesley.

Hyperthot. (n.d.). *Software Development Methodology.* Retrieved October 13, 2010, from Hyperthot: http/www.hyperthot.com

INTOSAI. (n.d.). *Working Group on IT Audit.* Retrieved October 9, 2010, from www.intosaiitaudit.org

Marcus, A. (2002). User-interface design, culture, and the future. *Proceedings of the Working Conference on Advanced Visual Interfaces,* 15-27.

Microsoft. (2009). *MSN Encarta.*

Moore, J. (2009, October 14). *Building a Buisness Case as the Foundation for Project Success.* Retrieved September 3, 2010, from ProjectSmart.co.uk:

http://www.projectsmart.co.uk/building-a-business-case-as-the-foundation-for-project-success.html

Pavlou, P. A., & Stewart, D. W. (2000, Fall). *Measuring the Effect and Effectiveness of Interactive Advertising: A Research Agenda*. Retrieved Septemeber 2010, 2010, from Journal of Interactive Advertisement: http://jiad.org/article6

PSFK. (2009). *Japan's Electronic Paper Advertising Poster*. Retrieved September 2010, from http://www.psfk.com/2009/07/japans-electronic-paper-advertising-poster.html

Rakkolainen, I., & Lugmayr, A. (2007). Immaterial Display for Interactive Advertisements. *ACM International Conference Proceeding Series; Vol. 203*, 95 - 98.

Search Software Quality. (n.d.). *Methodology*. Retrieved October 5, 2010, from Search Software Quality: www.searchsoftwarequality.techtarget.com/sDefinition/0,,sid92_gci519580,00.html

Technology for the World. (2010). *Electronic Advertising Signs: Can Your Business Use One*. Retrieved September 2010, from http://techlive.biz/2010/08/electronic-advertising-signs-can-your-business-use-one/.

Vakratsas, D., & Ambler, T. (1999). How Advertising Works: What Do We Really Know? *The Journal of Marketing, Vol. 63*, 26-43.

Zhang, P., Ma, J., & Sun, X. (2008). Intelligent Delivery of Interactive Advertisement Content. *Bell Labs Technical Journal archive. Volume 13 , Issue 3*.

# Appendix – I – Meeting minutes

Table 6: Meeting Minutes

| Week | Day | Date | Tasks |
|------|-----|------|-------|
| 2 | Friday | 30/07/2010 | • Identified research based tasks to complete<br>• Shared contact email<br>• Setup Sharepoint Workspaces |
| 3 | Friday | 6/08/2010 | • Added more contact email addresses to the list<br>• Identified a series of models to be completed based on weekly tutorials<br>• Setup dropbox account for collaboration replacing Sharepoint Workspaces |
| 4 | Friday | 13/08/2010 | • Reassigned some tasks as some team members were having problems with generating accurate models<br>• Helped walk through some usage of iTunes |
| 5 | Friday | 20/08/2010 | • Update on project process<br>• Identify issues with the current way of building models |
| 6 | Friday | 27/08/2010 | • General update on project process<br>• Assign tasks to finish and review document |

# Appendix – II - Advertisement Management Model

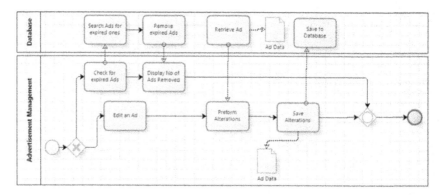

**Figure 21 Advertisement Management Model**

The Advertisement Management Model is an example model that shows how tools can be used by staff to modify the current systems in action. The first of the two shown is to check for expired advertisements. All advertisements have an expiry date and therefore a function is provided to make it easy to remove these items. Process-wise, a request is passed to the database to run the clean up operations. Once complete, a number of advertisements that have been removed are shown.

One other process shown is how the system handles editing an advertisement. It is assumed that the advertisement is already located within the database. A request is made to retrieve the advertisement, after which it can be edited. Once amendments have been completed, they are saved back to the database.

www.ingramcontent.com/pod-product-compliance
Lightning Source LLC
LaVergne TN
LVHW042303060326
832902LV00009B/1227